Birds in Our Back Yard
A Nature On Our Doorstep Book

Northern cardinal (female)

Annette Meredith

For Austin, Nina and Joe

With thanks to Michelle for all her help, to Ben and my brother Ian for their technical assistance
and to Ted for his ever-patient support and advice.
Thanks also to Dominic for his help and the author photo and to Alex for his input.

Pair of passenger pigeons depicted in mural at International Crane Foundation, Baraboo, Wisconsin.
The mural was created by Victor Bakhtin. (Courtesy Project Passenger Pigeon)

Copyright © 2015 Annette Meredith
All photographs copyright © 2015 Annette Meredith.
Many thanks to Linda Rainville for the photograph on page 1 of the cedar waxwing catching fruit.

All rights reserved.
ISBN-13: 978-1505378108
ISBN-10: 1505378109

Birds you'll find in this Book

Bluebird, Eastern	10, 11, 32, 36, 39
Cardinal, Northern	8, 10, 14, 15, 31, 36
Chickadee, Carolina	29
Crow, American	22
Dove, Mourning	17, 39
Duck, Mallard	34
Finch, House	11, 28
Finch, Purple	28
Flicker, Northern	20
Goldfinch, American	9, 12, 26, 27, 36
Hawk, Red-shouldered	3
Hawk, Sharp-shinned	3
Hummingbird, Ruby-throated	7, 9
Jay, Blue	23
Junco, Dark-eyed	16
Meadowlark, Eastern	5
Mockingbird, Northern	2, 32
Nuthatch, White-breasted	29, 32, 39
Robin, American	21, 31
Sapsucker, Yellow-bellied	6
Siskin, Pine	27
Sparrow, Chipping	10
Sparrow, House	25, 39
Sparrow, Song	36
Sparrow, White-throated	25
Starling, European	24
Thrasher, Brown	33, 39
Titmouse, Tufted	8, 30
Warbler, Pine	8
Waxwing, Cedar	1
Woodpecker, Downy	9, 19
Woodpecker, Pileated	20
Woodpecker, Red-bellied	18, 20
Woodpecker, Red-headed	18
Wren, Carolina	33

House finch

Ruby-throated Hummingbird

Pine warbler

Carolina **Wren**

Small flock of American Robins in winter

Part One – The Disappearing Birds

When we go outside, what do we usually hear? If we're in a park or back yard, one of the sounds is almost always the sound of birds. Even in towns, sparrows and pigeons and other birds peck around on the ground for food or perch on the rooftops and balance on wires. They sing or squawk, chatter or tweet, coo or caw. Imagine a world without the background noise of the birds. It would be very, very quiet.

Part of a flock of Cedar Waxwings

Size: just over 7"

Cedar Waxwing

Ecosystem –
A community of living and non-living things (water, soil, air, plants and everything living) that work together to create a balance. It can be big or small.

When we see plenty of birds, it tells us that the environment is probably healthy and safe for other creatures too. When there are not many birds, or fewer than there used to be, it may be an important sign telling us to look closely to see if there have been any changes in the local ecosystem. It may be vital to take action so that wildlife can survive. We can all help to protect birds, even if we only help those in our own back yards.

It's very easy to take birds for granted. We expect them to be there and we haven't always realized what can happen if they disappear. About fifty years ago, we began to notice the effect of pesticides on the environment, especially on birds. Since then, many organizations have been created to spread the message that we must protect the environment and everything in it. Today, that message is more important than ever.

Pesticide – a chemical substance or mixture that is designed to kill pests, but may also poison or kill other creatures.

A food chain starts with plant life and ends with animal life. Then when the animal dies, it goes back into the soil and feeds the plants, completing the circle of life.

The size of a bird is its length from the tip of its bill to the tip of its tail.

Size: about 10"

Northern Mockingbird

When pesticides are sprayed on plants, any creatures on the plants are poisoned. Those insects, caterpillars, spiders and other bugs are all food for birds and small mammals, which are in turn food for other creatures further up the food chain. Pesticides never stay just in the area where they are sprayed; they are carried into the environment and can be there for years.

Hawks are high up in the food chain. If one of these hawks catches a mouse that has eaten an insect or a seed poisoned by chemicals, it will be affected. Everything in nature is connected.

Red-shouldered Hawk

Size: between 18" and 22"

Sharp-shinned Hawk

Size: between 10" and 14"

Hawks have sharply pointed beaks. You can tell a lot about what a bird eats by looking at its bill.

Humans are at the top of the food chain. When pesticides are used, they are carried into the air, soil and water and they affect everything in the ecosystem, including people.

150 years ago, there were more passenger pigeons in North America than any other bird. Nobody believed that they could ever be in danger of extinction, because there were millions or even billions of them. They would travel together in flocks so large that they would darken the sky and they made such a loud noise that people outside would often run indoors! Always traveling and roosting in large groups made it very easy for people to catch them and kill them and lots of people hunted them to sell as meat. By 1900 there were only a few left and just over 100 years ago, in 1914, the last known passenger pigeon died at the Cincinnati zoo.

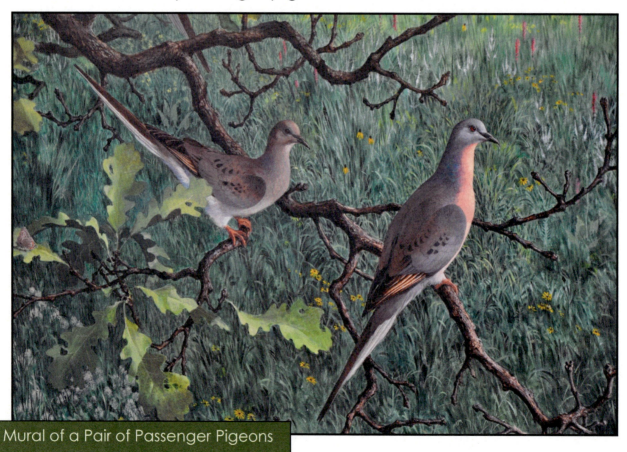

Mural of a Pair of Passenger Pigeons

Today, hundreds more species of birds are in danger. Some, like the passenger pigeon, have already become extinct, but others could still be saved if people take action to protect them.

Eastern Meadowlark

Size: about 9"

Habitat – a natural home.

Here are three eastern meadowlarks in their natural habitat. Birds that can only live in one kind of habitat are especially sensitive to changes in the environment. Meadowlarks feed mostly on insects found in a grassland habitat and so that's where they have to live. Many birds are losing their habitat because of human activity, including the clearing of land for construction and pollution of the environment by pesticides and herbicides. There are now only about a quarter as many eastern meadowlarks as there were forty years ago. Their numbers will go down even more if we don't make an effort to protect grasslands.

It is believed that as many as one out of every eight species of birds in the world is in danger of slipping towards extinction, unless we take more care of the environment and make sure that we don't upset the delicate balance of nature.

Part Two – If You Feed Them, They Will Come

It's very hard to sneak up on a bird. They have really good eyesight and hearing. If a bird sees any sudden movement or hears the slightest unusual sound, it will sound the alarm and every bird in the area will fly away and hide. Birds are always on the lookout and as soon as you open your back door, they will usually disappear. They are still there, you just won't see them. Most can blend in with their surroundings, and the shrubs and trees seem to swallow them up. The females are usually less colorful and have markings that mean they are easily camouflaged, but even brightly colored birds can sometimes seem to melt away.

Size: about 8"- 9"

Yellow-bellied Sapsucker

Despite the bright red patch on its head, this sapsucker (a type of woodpecker) is hard to see against the bark of the tree.

Camouflage – blending in with your surroundings so that you're hard to see.

Most birds are easily scared away, because they are always wary and on the lookout for predators. Open spaces mean danger to them and they like to have places to hide, like bushes, shrubs, trees and long grass.

Adult male

This hummingbird is well camouflaged when it perches on the stem of a cardinal vine.

Ruby-throated Hummingbird

Size: 3" to 3 ½"

Birds are attracted to back yards which have plants and trees that produce seeds and berries for them to eat, as well as places for them to perch and hide. Birds also need a source of water. The more you have that the birds need, the more birds you will bring to your back yard. Then all you have to do is find ways to bring them out into areas where you can see them, without putting them in danger from predators.

Predator – an animal or bird that kills and eats other creatures.

An easy way to attract more birds to your yard is to put out food and water for them. If you place feeders near a window, you will have a better chance of seeing the birds up close, although they may still see movement inside the house, so you'll need to be patient and sit quietly to watch them.

Tufted Titmouse

Northern Cardinal (female)

There are a lot of different kinds of bird feeders. Most of them are for seed and they attract seed-eaters like this northern cardinal and tufted titmouse. Some birds eat only seeds; they are the vegetarians of the bird world. Others will eat seeds and insects and some only eat insects or meat. Most backyard birds love sunflower seeds, so you can't go wrong filling a feeder with those (black oil are the best). If you hang out a suet cake as well, you'll attract insect eaters and have a greater variety of birds at feeders.

Pine Warbler — Size: about 5 ½"

Like their name suggests, pine warblers spend a lot of time among pine trees and are usually high up, so they are hard to spot. This pine warbler flew down to investigate a suet cake. It's always exciting when a more unusual bird visits the feeders. If you can't take a photo, try to remember details like a bird's color and size, and the shape of a bird's beak.

Hummingbirds are insect eaters, but they also eat nectar, which is why we can put out feeders with sugar-water just for them. People who live far enough south, especially on the west coast, are lucky enough to see hummingbirds at any time of year. If you live on the east coast, or further north, you will have to wait for spring.
Ruby-throated hummingbirds are regular visitors to feeders all through the summer, so it's definitely worth hanging out a feeder or two to attract them. Sometimes, other birds like to have a sip of something sweet, too!

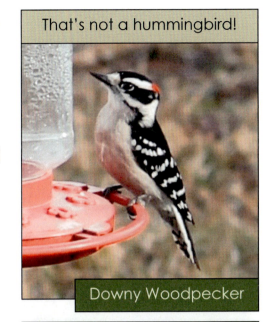

That's not a hummingbird!

Downy Woodpecker

Male Ruby-throated Hummingbird

American Goldfinches on sock feeder filled with nyjer seed

female

Top foods for attracting birds to your back yard:
* Black oil sunflower seeds
* Nyjer seed (sometimes known as thistle seed)
* White millet and cracked corn (but not if you
* Peanuts   have house sparrows)
* Meal worms (live or dried)
* Peanut butter (best if mixed with cornmeal)
* Suet cakes and birdseed balls
...and (for nectar lovers) sugar-water

Chipping Sparrows

Size: about 5"

It's important to hang feeders not only where you can see them, but also where it's safe for birds. They need to be able to fly quickly to a nearby bush or tree if they sense danger, so there should be places for them to perch and areas for them to hide. Make sure the feeders are far enough off the ground that cats and other predators can't reach them. Position them close to a window (three feet or less) because when they are placed further away, birds may fly straight into the reflection of the sky in the glass. Clean the feeders regularly so that you don't risk making the birds sick.

Birds will also be attracted to your back yard if you provide clean water for them. You can make your own birdbath from any shallow dish, or there are a lot of choices if you buy one. Birds usually visit birdbaths to drink the water. They also need water because they must keep their feathers clean. This cardinal is looking a bit bedraggled while he's fluffing up to dry off!

Bluebird couple taking a bath

There are three things that all birds need: food, water and shelter (or cover). We can provide these in lots of different ways and we don't have to spend a lot of money to do it. This bluebird is enjoying a shower under the spray of a hose and is being watered along with the plants!
If you're watering the garden, watch to see which birds come for a bath.

Size: about 7"

Eastern Bluebird

In summer, the ground dries quickly and the birds need water more than ever.
In winter, water often freezes and so putting out some warm water for birds to drink may make all the difference to them. Winter time is also when they are most in need of the food that we can give them.

Once you start watching the birds and helping them to survive by providing them with food, water and shelter, you'll be rewarded with more and more birds coming to your back yard. Soon, you'll learn to tell them apart, you'll find out what they like to eat, and you'll know their names.

Female House Finch

Size: about 5"

Part Three – Let's Meet Some Feathered Friends

Let's take a look at some of the birds you might see from your window, in your back yard, or in the park.

Birds move around a lot, and many migrate. Even when they don't, they may move to different areas in their search for food. If you make them welcome they may choose to live in your back yard, but some of the birds will only be around at certain times of year. Some birds will be with you in spring and summer; others will arrive as the summer migrants leave in fall.

The seasons bring big changes to everyone's backyard. Not only do we see different birds at different times of year, but the birds themselves sometimes look very different, depending on the season.

Molt – to replace all or part of a bird's feathers by growing new ones.

Birds' feathers wear out. They have to be replaced regularly and most birds molt at least once a year. The male goldfinches look the same as the females in winter, but when spring is around the corner they molt and grow new, beautiful, bright yellow feathers.

American Goldfinch

While they are molting and new feathers are growing, their colors can look rather strange and blotchy.

Migration – the movement of animals, birds, fish or insects from one place to another at different times of year, usually depending on the season.

When you start to watch the birds in your back yard, you have to learn how to identify the birds that you see. To begin with, birds may sometimes all look the same to you, but if you're a good detective you'll soon learn their names and see how different they really are. Start by collecting clues.

Where did you see the bird? On the ground, in a tree?

What was it doing? Was it eating? If so, what?

What was its main color? Any other colors?

Did it have any speckles, stripes, or patches of color?

How big was it? Did it have a long or short tail?

What shape was its beak?

Did it have any unusual features?

Did you hear it sing, or make any sounds?

Was it by itself, or with another bird or birds?

Forage – to search for food over a wide area.

Some birds forage for food on the ground. You'll often see them scratching in the grass or fallen leaves as they look for insects, grubs and seeds. Other birds are more usually seen in trees, on plants, or at feeders. Woodpeckers and nuthatches are often seen on tree trunks, probing for insects under the bark. Birds like swifts and swallows catch insects in the air as they fly.

Northern Cardinal

The cardinal is an easy bird to recognize. Sometimes known as a redbird, the bright and cheerful cardinal likes visiting feeders, and it's easily spotted as it perches on branches and sings a song to let other birds know that this is its territory. In spring, the males and females often sing to each other. Although you won't see one if you live in the Northwest, it's the state bird of seven states and can be found in all the eastern and some southern states.

Territory – an area to be defended. It usually includes a food source and may also include a nesting site.

Size: about 8" to 9"

Northern Cardinal - male

In winter, the males are especially easy to spot, with their bright red plumage against the bare trees. They have a crest which is sometimes flattened, but usually stands up in a peak, and the black mask around their orange bills makes them look a bit like bandits!

During the winter cardinals often gather in small flocks, but both the males and females become very territorial in spring and have even been known to fight their own reflections in a window!

Plumage – a bird's feathers.

Northern Cardinal - female

Brood – a family of young birds.

The same bird can look quite different, depending on the light.

Female cardinals are an olive green-brown instead of red, but they still have tinges of red on their wings, tail and crest. In spring, you may see the male feeding the female at a feeder. Cardinals often mate for life.
If you see the red male, look around and you will probably spy a female. Cardinals like to forage on the ground for seeds and insects. They will come to feeders and can also be seen hunting for fallen seed on the ground beneath the feeders. Like many birds, cardinals will often have more than one brood each year. Sunflower seeds are their favorite food at feeders and their fledglings will sometimes follow them and sit begging for food on nearby branches, or even on the feeders themselves. You can recognize young birds by their tufty plumage and yellow gape when they open their bills. It's fun when you see a parent feeding one of its fledglings.

Fledge – to leave the nest after growing flight feathers.
Fledgling – a young bird that has just left the nest and learned to fly.

Dark-eyed Junco

Dark-eyed juncos are winter visitors to a lot of backyards. They look a bit like someone has held them and dipped them in white paint, as they have a dividing line between their slate gray tops and white belly below.

Dark-eyed Junco – male

Size: about 6"

Juncos like to be together and they don't mind other birds joining them as they forage, either. You'll often see them with sparrows, doves or bluebirds as they search for seeds.

Females are a soft brownish-gray, rather than the slate gray, almost black coloring of the male.

Seed-eaters like juncos and other sparrows prefer small seeds.

During the nesting season, they will also eat insects.

Dark-eyed Junco – female

Juncos have white outer tail feathers that spread out in flight. Look for the white flash as they fly.

Mourning Dove

Mourning Dove
Size: just over 12"

Mourning doves are common birds across most of the country throughout the year. They are seed eaters and are often seen in groups in winter, foraging near feeders for fallen seed.

Listen for their soft, sad coo and for the whistling, whirring sound of their wings when they fly. If you see a bird that looks very similar but has a dark ring around the back of its neck instead of a cheek spot, you've sighted a Eurasian collared dove.
Don't confuse doves with the much larger pigeons, often seen in towns.
Mourning doves are shy birds that are easily spooked, but they sometimes nest close to people in places like gutters on houses, or in hanging baskets of flowers.

Woodpeckers

Male | Female
Red-bellied Woodpecker
Size: just over 9"

Can you see the difference between the male and female woodpecker? The female doesn't have as much red on her head; it's mostly gray. You might think that this woodpecker looks like it should be called a red-headed rather than a red-bellied woodpecker, but that name was already taken. Red-headed woodpeckers really do have a completely red head! Both these woodpeckers are found in the eastern half of the country, but the red-bellied is more common. The red belly is more of a faintly pink belly!

Red-headed woodpecker
Size: about 9"

Look for woodpeckers on the trunks or branches of trees, or sometimes on the ground hunting for insects. If you live near woods, you may hear the sound of drumming, but it could be any of the species of woodpecker, so that's when a good pair of binoculars is useful.

These are both males.
Female downy woodpeckers don't have a little red patch on their heads.

Downy Woodpecker   Size: about 6"

Downy woodpeckers are our smallest woodpecker, and they are also the most common.
They are small enough to perch on plant stems and to move around on slender tree branches, looking like little acrobats as they hang upside down to search for insects beneath the bark.
They will come to feeders for sunflowers seeds and as you can see, they love suet too!

If you see a woodpecker that looks like a downy woodpecker but is about the size of a robin and has a much longer bill, you've probably come across a hairy woodpecker.

The pileated woodpecker also has red on its head, but you won't mistake it for any other woodpecker if you see or hear it – it's huge! When it drums on wood, the sound echoes through the trees. It has a large and very powerful beak for making holes bigger, for drumming to announce its presence and communicate, or for chipping away the bark on trees as it hunts for insects.

The male has a red mustache.

Size: about 19"

Male Pileated Woodpecker

You would think that woodpeckers would get a headache from rapping on wood, but they have thick skulls and strong neck muscles so that they can hammer on trees without hurting themselves.

The holes that woodpeckers make in trees are often later used by other birds, as well as creatures like bats.

Downy and red-bellied woodpeckers are the most common at feeders, but when you visit a park with lots of trees, look and listen for other woodpeckers.

Size: about 12". Northern flickers are the only woodpeckers to feed mainly on the ground.

Red-bellied Woodpecker and Northern Flicker

Woodpeckers use their tongues to get to their food, which is usually insects but can be seeds, berries, nuts or even tree sap. They often have sticky or barbed tongues, which help them to extract insects from beneath the bark.

American Robin

In spring, American robins are often seen on lawns, tugging worms out of the ground.
They can be found year round in many parts of the US, although some fly north to breeding grounds in Canada for the summer.
In winter, they gather in large flocks and spend much of the day in trees, looking for berries.

American Robin

Size: about 8" to 11"

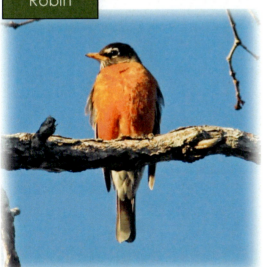

American robins eat worms, insects and berries. Because they like to forage on lawns for worms, they are vulnerable to pesticide poisoning.
Their rusty, red-orange chest makes them easy to recognize and in early spring they are often the first birds to sing their beautiful songs at dawn.
Their eggs are such a pretty blue that they have a crayon color named after them, "Robin's egg blue".

There are many Native American stories about robins.
Perhaps the best known legend is that the robin got its red breast when it saved the life of a man and his son by fanning the flames of a camp fire to keep them warm.

American Crow

In Aesop's fable "The Crow and The Pitcher", the crow cleverly works out how to drink from a jug of water. He can't reach the water with his big beak, but by dropping pebbles into the pitcher, the water level rises high enough for him to be able to drink.

American Crow
Size: about 18"

Crows are big birds and easy to recognize by sight or sound. You won't normally see just one crow; American crows like to gather in flocks, especially in winter. Even if you don't see them, you can often hear them; their rasping, hoarse "caw" is loud and very distinctive. They will come to back yards to eat scraps, seeds and suet, but they are ground foragers and too big to eat from feeders. You will see them throughout the year in most states, although some leave for breeding grounds in the northern states and Canada in the summer. Crows are intelligent and good at solving problems. Have you ever heard the story of the crow and the pitcher?

Blue Jay

Blue Jay
Size: about 12"

Blue jays are not found along the west coast, but they are common in the rest of the country. They love acorns and can often be seen hopping around in oak trees in winter, or on the ground hunting for insects.
Their favorite foods at feeders are peanuts, sunflower seeds and suet.
Blue jays have a noisy call and are good mimics. Sometimes they will imitate the sound of a hawk's piercing cry as they approach a feeder.
It frightens other birds away, leaving the food just for them!
Like crows, blue jays are clever and good at problem solving.

Birds with blue feathers like blue jays look blue only because the light shining on them reflects off the feathers. This type of blue is called a structural color. If you let light pass through a feather from behind rather than shining on it, it doesn't look blue any more.

European Starling

Starlings like to travel around together most of the year and are often seen in a noisy flock perched high in trees, on buildings or wires, or on the ground looking for food.

Iridescent – shining with many different colors from different angles.

Size: about 7" to 8"

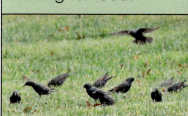

Starlings and sparrows can be aggressive, driving out native species which would otherwise have used nest boxes intended for them.

Every starling in America is descended from only one hundred which were brought here from Europe and released in New York's Central Park in 1890. Back then, no-one knew how risky it is to introduce a species into a new environment. Starlings will eat almost anything and they can be a nuisance at feeders; many people consider them a pest. In the warmer months they eat mainly insects, worms and caterpillars. They are quite easy to identify, with their iridescent summer plumage and speckled winter feathers. Starlings often gather in large, noisy flocks. At times, hundreds or even thousands of them congregate and swoop and swirl in the air together. When they fly in tight formation like this, seeming to move as one, it's called a murmuration of starlings and it's an unforgettable sight.

Many species of birds have very descriptive collective nouns for groups of them. Some of the best known are a murder of crows, a charm of finches, a gaggle of geese, a parliament of owls, a host of sparrows and an exultation of skylarks.

House Sparrow

House sparrows are common on all continents except Antarctica and are probably one of the best-known birds, because they like living close to people. There were no house sparrows in America until some were brought from England in the 1850s, so they are the only non-native sparrows.

Sometimes you'll see them hopping around under outdoor tables at restaurants, or pecking at spilled birdseed in the garden section of a store. Most sparrows prefer seeds, but they will also eat insects and fruit.

male
Size: about 6"

female

There are at least 35 species of sparrow in North America and they can be quite hard to tell apart, as they are mostly small, brown birds that look alike at first glance. Look for differences like color or pattern markings and size.

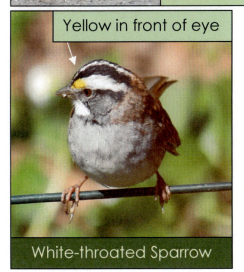
Yellow in front of eye
White-throated Sparrow

In 1958 the leader of China, Chairman Mao, ordered that sparrows should be killed because they ate the seeds of crops in the fields. What the Chinese didn't realize was that sparrows eat insects and also feed them to their young. When the grain grew, the sparrows were not there to control the insects, which ate and damaged the crops. Many people died in the famine that followed.
The sparrow population gradually recovered, but the Chinese had paid a terrible price. They learned that the balance of nature can be very delicate.

American Goldfinch

All finches love seeds so if you hang out tube or sock feeders with nyjer seed in them, you'll attract American goldfinches. They are small, pretty birds that love to hang out together and are fun to watch as they squabble with each other over the seed at feeders.

The males are easy to identify in spring and summer, when they are as bright as canaries.
In the winter, they are hard to tell apart from the females, as they look almost the same.

Size: about 5"

If you live in southern or western states, you'll probably only see goldfinches in winter. They still have black with white barring on their wings and some yellow feathers around their beaks, but they look very different with their mostly pale, gray-brown feathers. Finches of all kinds flock to feeders, especially in winter.

American Goldfinch in winter

American Goldfinch (three males)

sunflowers

Pine siskins are finches that come to feeders for nyjer seed. They have yellow on their wings, but their chests are speckled.

Pine Siskin

All finches like sunflower seeds, so growing sunflowers is an easy way to attract them. Look carefully, and you'll find three bright yellow goldfinches searching for seeds in the sunflower patch. The goldfinch in the photo below is a female and in summer she is a greenish color rather than yellow.

Goldfinches nest later than other birds. They wait for milkweed and thistle to produce seeds, which they use in their nests and as food for the young birds. Many seed-eating birds feed insects to their chicks, but goldfinches are true vegetarians and eat only seeds.

Goldfinches have a bouncy flight pattern and often twitter as they fly.

House Finch

Finches visiting flower seed heads

House Finch

House finches used to be seen only in western states, but in the middle of the twentieth century some were released in New York and now they can be found across most of the country. They come to feeders for seeds and scraps and they also like to visit birdbaths. Groups of them often gather in winter and set up a cheerful, noisy twittering. The male is a warm red color mixed with white-edged gray wings, but the female is quite plain and is often mistaken for a sparrow. Look for the chunky finch bill.

House Finch — female — male — Size: just over 5"

House finches are small birds that like to flock together. They will sometimes gather in large groups and you will find that if one comes to your feeders, more will follow!

In the winter you may see purple finches, which look very similar. Look for ways in which they are different.

Purple Finches

Carolina Chickadee

Chickadees are inquisitive birds that are often the first to find a feeder. They usually pluck a seed from the feeder and then retreat to the nearest tree to eat it. They also like to hide a lot of seeds for later and are good at remembering where they hid them, even though they tuck each seed in a different place. In the north and west you will see black-capped chickadees and in the south, Carolina chickadees. They look almost the same and are hard to tell apart, but their songs and calls are different.

Chickadees are like tiny acrobats as they move around on branches and twigs hunting for insects. If you see a similar bird running head-first down the trunk of a tree, you may have seen a nuthatch, like this one scampering down the tree with a seed.

Size: about 4" to 5"

Carolina Chickadee

White-breasted Nuthatch

Size: about 5" to 6"

Chickadees and nuthatches like to cram seeds under bark, hiding them for later.

Tufted Titmouse

You will often see a tufted titmouse at a feeder, where they will snatch a sunflower seed and fly with it to a nearby branch. Watch them as they hammer the seed with their beak to break open the shell. Like chickadees, they will hoard seeds in secret hiding places. They are common all over the country, but are not usually seen in the mountains. In the summer, they mostly eat caterpillars, spiders, snails and insects like ants and wasps.

Size: about 6"

Tufted Titmouse

They are cavity nesters, but they can't make their own holes in trees, so they often use holes made by woodpeckers and they will also nest in bird boxes.

Tufted titmice like to line their nests with soft fur. They have even been known to pluck hair from a sleeping animal! If you have a furry pet, brush it and hook the fur on twigs in spring for the birds.

Part Four – Birds and the Seasons

When it's cold outside, we can wrap up snugly or stay indoors, but birds have to find ways to stay warm through the winter months if they are to survive. Some have to migrate to escape the cold, but a lot of birds are well adapted to deal with the challenges that winter brings, as long as they can find clean water and enough food to give them energy and warmth.

In many parts of the country, January and February mean long, cold nights with temperatures often below freezing. It's at this time of year that taking care of backyard birds by providing food and water for them can save their lives. If you provide shelter as well, they will probably stay. You may even be rewarded with seeing them raise their families when spring arrives.

This robin has one leg tucked under its feathers for warmth.

Male and female cardinal

Birds have several ways to stay warm in winter. Many birds grow extra feathers when they molt in fall, and their outer feathers are waterproof. Look carefully at this cardinal and you'll see that it has fluffed up the downy, insulating feathers that grow close to its body. Birds' legs and feet are covered with special scales to reduce heat loss and birds shiver to generate body heat. They also eat more in fall so they can build up body fat to help keep them warm through the winter.

Spring starts early for birds. Birds that stay year round will have been investigating birdhouses during the winter months and by February many have chosen their nesting site. Migrating birds start to arrive and suddenly our back yards are alive with song and color again. Spring is a time for finding a mate, nesting and raising families. If you wake early enough in the morning, you may hear the "dawn chorus". The birds that have survived the winter now normally enjoy a time of plenty, with insects emerging, flowers blooming and warmer temperatures signaling that winter is over.

A Bluebird Family

Four babies hatch from the sky blue eggs in the nest box put up for the bluebirds. Both parents feed the chicks – in the photo you can see the father – and in the last picture one of the fledglings is leaving the nest, with a nuthatch looking on!

Young Bluebird

Fledglings often have mottled feathers to help camouflage them.
Young birds rely on their parents to feed them even after they have left the nest, until they learn to find food for themselves.

Mockingbird fledgling and parent

Birds such as bluebirds, chickadees and titmice are cavity nesters and they may nest in boxes we put out for them. Other birds, like this brown thrasher, build their nests high in the branches of trees.

Some birds choose to nest near people. House sparrows will often nest close to buildings, or even in them. Wrens seem to prefer looking for unusual nesting places. This Carolina wren found an old flowerpot and decided it was a great place to build a nest!

Size: about 11"

Brown Thrasher

Carolina Wren

Carolina wren fledgling

Tiny wrens can sing very loudly!

Size: about 5"

Birds often have more than one brood in a year. Many fledglings don't survive and those that do still have dangers to face every day. This young chipping sparrow has to hide in the tall grass until it can learn to fly properly and feed itself. When baby birds first leave the nest, they are very vulnerable. We should always move quietly near nests and never disturb nesting birds.

In spring and summer you may see young birds and wonder what they are, because they often look very different from their parents. The parents may look different from each other, too. Usually, young birds and females are less brightly colored. Being camouflaged protects them from predators.

Mallard ducks
Female
Male

You've probably seen ducks in parks. Here is the first duck egg in a nest near a pond. Ducks usually have large families, because many young ones don't survive. Ducklings learn to swim before they can fly. Look at how different the adult male and female mallard ducks are.

As summer moves into fall, birds start to move on. Some will stay in the same area, and some families will even stay together through the winter, but most birds move around a lot more than we realize. It's during spring and fall that we see the biggest movement of birds as they migrate, and at those times we may see birds that aren't normally in our back yards. Look up into the skies in fall and you may see and hear flocks of migrating geese flying in a "V" formation. Many birds travel along the coasts and waterways and some birds prefer to fly at night during migration. Occasionally, a flock of birds will descend on a back yard if they see berries or other food.

Part Five – What Would We Do Without Birds?

Throughout history, birds have played an important role in people's lives. During the Revolutionary and Civil Wars and also in the two World Wars of the last century, homing pigeons were used for carrying messages that brought information which saved many people's lives. Some of the pigeons became quite famous and flew numerous flights into enemy territory. Birds were the inspiration for us to build machines so that we too can fly, although an airplane cannot match the amazing aerial abilities of a bird. A bird's wings act as both wing and propeller, so it can fly in a much more complicated and varied way than a plane. Different species of birds have different types of wings, from short wings for quick upward movement to long, broad wings for gliding and soaring.

Canaries, parrots, parakeets and cockatiels are all birds that some people like to keep as pets.
Birds and their eggs have always been an important source of food for people across the world.
Bird feathers have been used for decoration and also for warmth in quilts and clothing. Flight feathers of larger birds can be quills and were used for writing before the invention of pens. Even bird dung, called guano, can be useful; it's been valued as a fertilizer for centuries. Birds have also been an inspiration to artists and scientists since the dawn of civilization.

Pet Canary

"Canary in a coal mine"- canaries were taken into coal mines so that miners would know that the air was safe to breathe. If the canary stopped singing, they knew that there were poisonous gases that could kill them if they didn't get out straight away. If something or someone is like "a canary in a coal mine", it means that they are giving an early warning of danger to others.

Birds are an essential part of the ecosystem. They pollinate plants, spread seeds and control insect populations by eating bugs. They are part of the food chain as both predators and prey.

Their usefulness to humans as ecological indicators is vital, which means that we need them because watching and studying them tells us a lot about our environment and makes us take notice of problems.

Increasingly, birds are an important source of ecotourism. We don't have to travel to faraway places to enjoy birds, though, because we all have birds in our own back yards and can easily attract more of them. Look out of your window today and see if you can identify a bird!

Male Cardinal at seed feeder

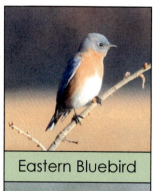
Eastern Bluebird

Goldfinch

Song Sparrow singing

Ecotourism – "Environmentally responsible travel to natural areas, in order to enjoy and appreciate nature" (International Union for Conservation of Nature, or IUCN).

Nature Notes

Check the boxes when you've identified the birds. You can also add the date and where they were seen. Once you've learned to identify these common birds, you can truly say you have become a birdwatcher!

Things You Can Do

Start by putting out food and water for the birds. With patience, some of the birds may learn to trust you so that they don't all fly away as soon as you open the door. Always respect your birds' privacy, though, and try not to frighten or disturb them when they are feeding, drinking or bathing.
If you see a young bird on the ground, don't approach it; a parent is almost certainly close by, looking after it.

A pair of binoculars will help you to see a bird in much greater detail so that you'll be able to identify it more easily. Taking photos can also help to show more of the details that make birds look different from each other.
Soon, you'll discover that birds have different personalities, too!

There are many organizations for birdwatchers which are fun to join and lots of information is available online if you want to learn more about a particular bird. Becoming a birdwatcher has never been easier!

Black-eyed Susan
Coneflower

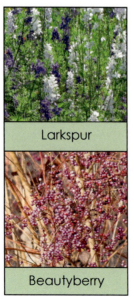
Larkspur
Beautyberry

Zinnia
Cosmos

If you have the space, ask if you can plant some sunflowers in your back yard and later in the year you will have fun watching lots of seed-eating birds cling to the seed heads as they enjoy the feast you have grown for them.
Here are some other plants that are easy to grow that will attract birds, bees and butterflies.

Make a list of the birds you have seen. If you draw pictures, they will help you to remember a bird's color and markings. Make a note of where and when the bird was sighted. Keep a nature diary and you will know when you're likely to see all the different birds next year, too.

Brown Thrasher

Nuthatch with suet

Feeders are the best way to provide food like sunflower and nyjer seed. In winter, birds need a lot more energy. Foods such as suet and peanuts provide the calories they need. Even in spring and summer, it's useful for parent birds to have an easy source of food to give them energy.

House Sparrow

Mourning Doves

Water attracts many more birds. There are birdbaths you can buy, but it's easy to make your own. This is an old flowerpot saucer filled with water, set on top of a large, upside-down flowerpot.

In early spring, put out nesting material like twigs, hair, fur, cotton batting, straw and short pieces of string. Mix clay soil and water in an old dish and leave it out, as some birds like to use mud when building their nests.

Muddy clay soil

Put up a nesting box in a sheltered place, out of direct sunlight (east-facing is good) and safe from predators. Try to place it where you can see it from a window. Happy birding!

Eastern Bluebirds (male in flight)

ABOUT THE AUTHOR

Annette Meredith is a master gardener, photographer and lifelong student of nature who is passionate about environmental issues and conservation. She was born in England but now lives in North Carolina, where she enjoys encouraging, observing and photographing nature as she works to improve sixty acres of woodland, meadows and organic gardens.

Other books in the "Nature on Our Doorstep" series:

Saving the Bees
Nature on Our Doorstep
The Secret World of Flowers

Helping the Hummingbirds
Butterflies are Beautiful

And for younger children:

Five First Rhyming Readers

Three First readers

Made in the USA
San Bernardino, CA
27 July 2016